Brilliant French Information Books, Level 1

6 Non-fiction Texts for Beginning Learners in Primary School

Danièle Bourdais and Sue Finnie

> For instructions on how to download your free audio files and printable resources for the stories, please see page 60.

Contents
1. La France en couleurs 1
2. Un, deux, trois, soleil ! 11
3. Des animaux importants 21
4. Bonjour tout le monde ! 31
5. Les jours de la semaine 41
6. C'est ça Paris ! 51

Downloadable files
The downloadable files include an audio recording of each reading book (eg. BFI1-1-BOOK-AUDIO.mp3), a PDF of each book (BFI1-1-BOOK-PDF.pdf as well as a pdf file containing the teacher book for Level 1 (BFI1-TB-PDF.pdf)

Published by Brilliant Publications Limited, Unit 10, Sparrow Hall Farm, Edlesborough, Dunstable, LU6 2ES.
www.brilliantpublications.co.uk
The name 'Brilliant Publications' is a registered trade mark.

Written by Danièle Bourdais and Sue Finnie
© Danièle Bourdais, Sue Finnie and Brilliant Publications Limited
Audio recording by Danièle Bourdais and Audrey Bourdais Paull
ISBN printed book: 978-1-78317-398-3
ISBN PDF book: 978-1-78317-401-0

First printed and published in the UK as 6 individual books in 2016. First printed and published in this collection in 2025.

The right of Danièle Bourdais and Sue Finnie to be identified as the authors of this work has been asserted by themselves in accordance with the Copyright, Designs and Patents Act 1988.

All rights reserved. Apart from any use permitted under UK copyright law, no part of this publication may be reproduced or transmitted in any form or by any means, electronic or mechanical, including photocopying and recording, or held within any information storage and retrieval system, without permission in writing from the publishers or under licence from the Copyright Licensing Agency Limited. Further details of such licenses (for reprographic reproduction) may be obtained from the Copyright Licensing Agency Limited, 5th Floor, Shackleton House, 4 Battle Bridge Lane, London SE1 2HX (https://cla.co.uk).

La France en couleurs

bleu

C'est **bleu** comme la mer Méditerranée.

blanc

C'est **blanc** comme
les montagnes des Alpes.

rouge

C'est **rouge** comme les fraises du marché.

noir

C'est **noir** comme les olives de Provence.

vert

C'est **vert** comme les raisins de Bordeaux.

jaune

C'est **jaune** comme
les champs de tournesols.

gris

C'est **gris** comme les toits de Paris.

As-tu bonne mémoire ?

1. Le raisin, c'est ...

   a) rouge
   b) jaune
   c) noir
   d) vert

2. Le tournesol, c'est ...

   a) bleu
   b) jaune
   c) vert
   d) rouge

3. Tu vois quelles couleurs ?

   a) blanc
   b) bleu
   c) vert
   d) rouge

4. En Normandie, les toits sont gris comme à Paris.

   a) vrai
   b) faux

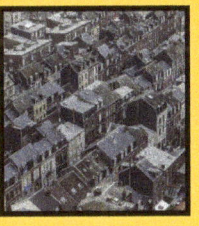

Quelle est ta couleur préférée ?
Le bleu ? Le blanc ? Le rouge ?

Un, deux, trois … soleil !

Je m'appelle Julie.

Voici mes photos de vacances.

un

Il y a **un** château de sable.

deux

Il y a **deux** garçons sur les toboggans.

trois

Il y a **trois** enfants à vélo.

quatre

Il y a **quatre** chiens sur la plage.

cinq

Il y a **cinq** personnes sur des kayaks.

six

Il y a <u>six</u> parfums différents:
<u>un</u>, <u>deux</u>, <u>trois</u>, <u>quatre</u>, <u>cinq</u>, <u>six</u> !

As-tu bonne mémoire ?

1. Il y a combien de kayaks ?

   a) deux
   b) trois
   c) six
   d) cinq

2. Il y a combien de garçons ?

   a) cinq
   b) un
   c) quatre
   d) deux

3. Il y a combien de chiens ?

   a) un
   b) quatre
   c) cinq
   d) deux

4. Il y a combien de parfums différents ?

   a) six
   b) cinq
   c) trois
   d) un

J'adore les vacances ! Et toi ?

Des animaux importants

le coq

C'est un symbole national en France.

le lion

C'est un symbole national en Belgique.

l'ours

C'est un symbole national en Suisse.

le castor

C'est un symbole national au Canada.

l'éléphant

C'est un symbole national en Côte d'Ivoire.

la tortue

C'est un symbole national au Vietnam.

l'aigle

C'est un symbole national aux États-Unis.

As-tu bonne mémoire ?

1. C'est ...

   a) la tortue
   b) l'aigle
   c) le coq

2. Le symbole de la France ?

   a) le coq
   b) l'ours
   c) le lion

3. Le lion, c'est un symbole national ...

   a) aux États-Unis
   b) en France
   c) en Belgique

4. Quel animal n'est pas un symbole national en Europe ?

   a) le lion
   b) l'éléphant
   c) l'ours

Et dans ton pays, quel animal est symbole national ?

Les jours de la semaine

lundi

<u>Lundi</u>, c'est le jour de la Lune.

mardi

Mardi, c'est le jour de Mars.

mercredi

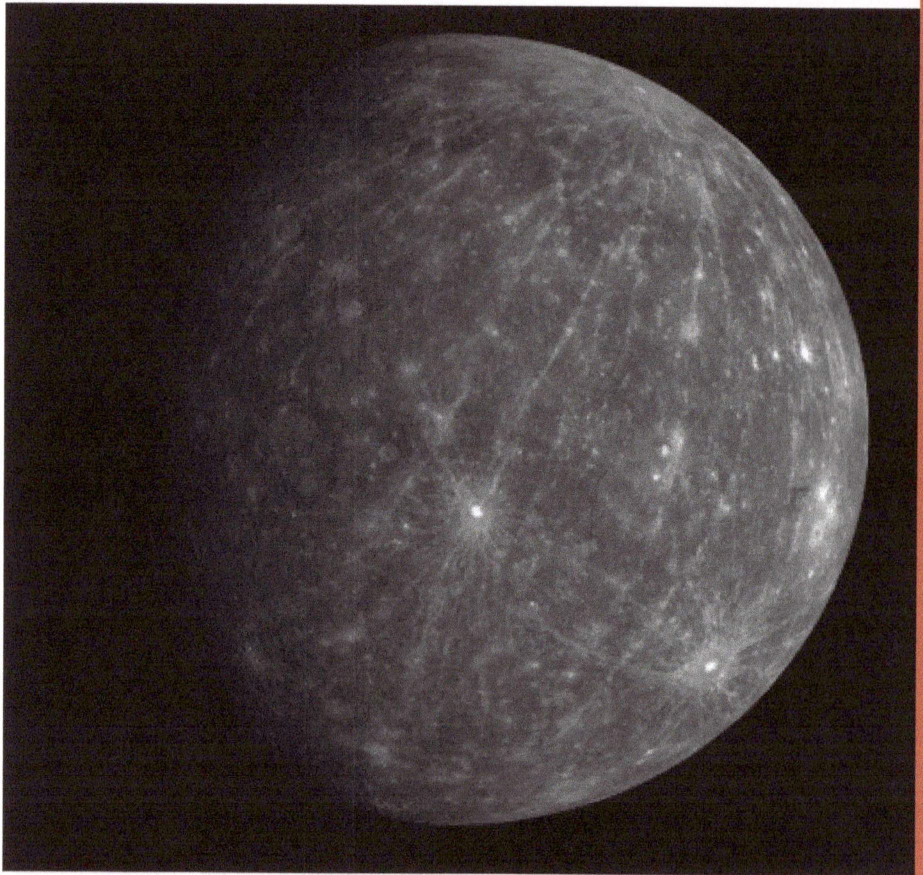

Mercredi, c'est le jour de Mercure.

jeudi

Jeudi, c'est le jour de Jupiter.

vendredi

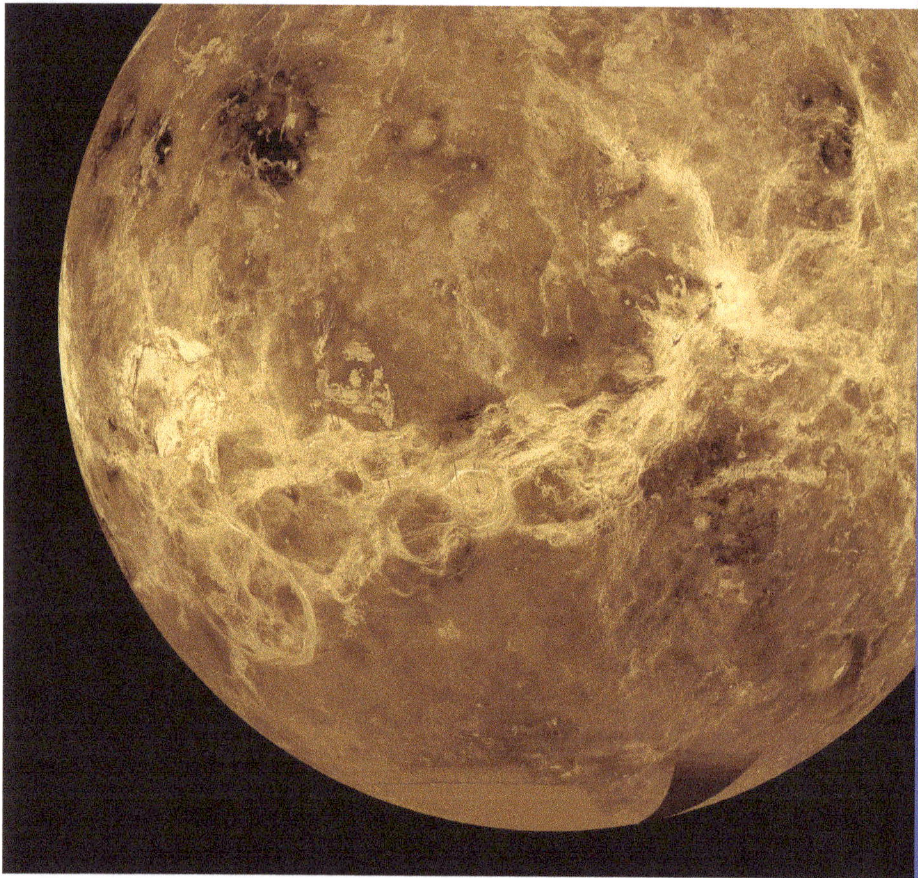

Vendredi, c'est le jour de Vénus.

samedi

Samedi, c'est le jour du Sabbat.

dimanche

<u>Dimanche</u>, c'est le jour de Dieu.

As-tu bonne mémoire ?

1. C'est quel jour ?

   a) vendredi
   b) lundi
   c) mercredi

2. En français, samedi, c'est le jour de Saturne ?

   a) oui
   b) non

3. Dimanche, c'est le jour ?

   a) du Soleil
   b) de Dieu

4. Quel jour pour Mars ?

   a) mardi
   b) mercredi

Et dans ta langue, c'est quoi l'origine des noms des jours de la semaine ?

Bonjour, tout le monde !

Dans différents pays …

on dit « bonjour »
de différentes façons.

En France ...

on se serre la main ou
on se fait la bise.

Au Japon …

on s'incline très bas.

En Inde …

on joint les mains.

Chez les Inuits …

on se frotte le nez.

Au Tibet ...

on tire la langue.

Et pour dire « au revoir » ...

on fait un geste avec la main.

As-tu bonne mémoire ?

1. Pour dire bonjour en Inde ...

   a) on joint les mains
   b) on tire la langue
   c) on se fait la bise

2. Traditionnellement, chez les Inuits ...

   a) on se serre la main
   b) on s'incline très bas
   c) on se frotte le nez

3. Au Japon, on s'incline très bas.

   a) vrai
   b) faux

4. Au Tibet, pour dire bonjour, on tire ...

   a) la langue
   b) le nez
   c) la main

Dans ton pays, qu'est-ce qu'on fait pour dire bonjour ?

C'est ça, Paris !

Viens, on visite la ville de Paris !
La Tour Eiffel …

c'est haut.

L'avenue des Champs-Élysées …

c'est long.

Le quartier de Montmartre ...

c'est vieux.

Le musée du Centre Pompidou …

c'est moderne.

Le Château de Versailles …

c'est beau.

La promenade en bateau sur la Seine …

c'est intéressant.

La visite des Catacombes …

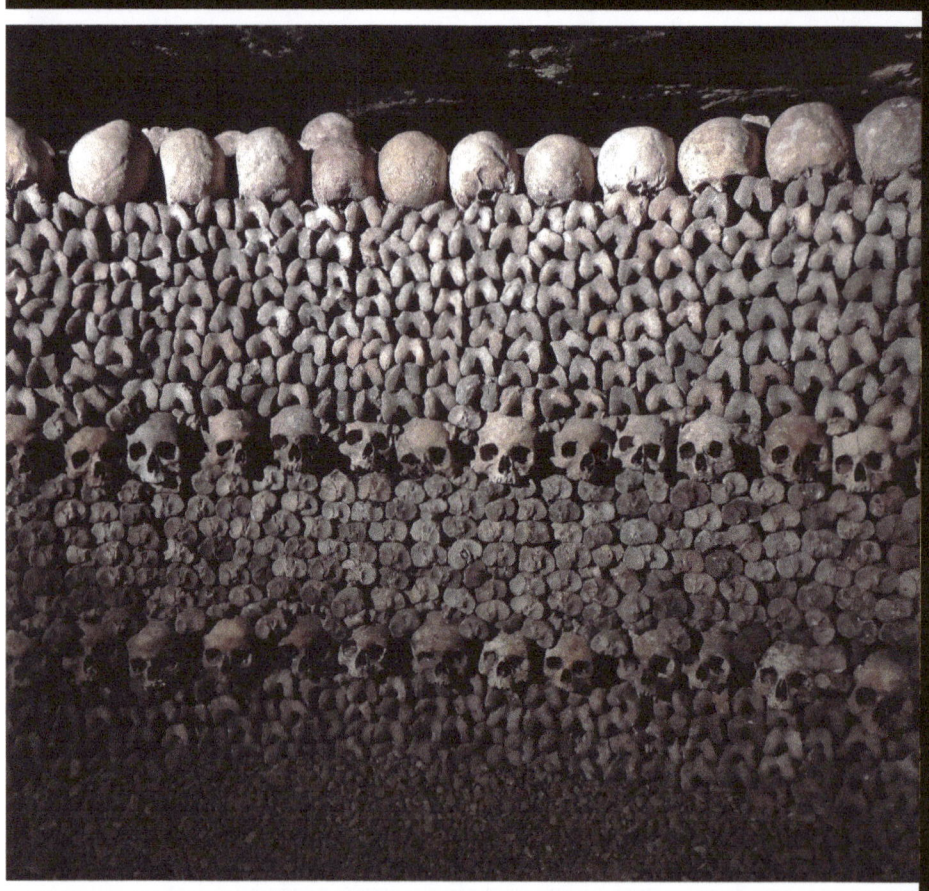

c'est … étonnant !

As-tu bonne mémoire ?

1. Le Centre Pompidou, c'est …

   a) moderne
   b) vieux

2. C'est haut ! C'est …

   a) la Tour Eiffel
   b) Versailles
   c) les Catacombes

3. Les Catacombes, c'est moderne.

   a) vrai
   b) faux

4. Le Sacré-Cœur à Montmartre, c'est …

   a) moderne
   b) long
   c) haut

Paris, c'est génial !
Et ta ville, c'est comment ?

Download instructions

To download your free resources for **Brilliant French Information Books, Level 1**.

Go to: **https://www.brilliantpublications.education**

You will need to set up a log in with an email address and password if you do not already have one for the https://www.brilliantpublications.education website. (Please note: you will need to set up a new account on this website to download your files, even if you already have an account on our main website.)

Your username may contain: letters, numbers and the special characters * - _ . @

You will be asked to confirm your email address by clicking the validation link emailed to you when you register. Don't forget to check in spam/junk if you do not see an email from us.

We have introduced 2-factor authorisation on this website to make it more secure. This means that whenever you log in, you will be sent a numerical authorisation code by email which you must copy and paste into the welcome page on the website. The authentication code only lasts 1 hour.

Once logged on, choose the **French** category and click on the cover for **Brilliant French Information Books, Level 1**.

Your unique password for the downloads is: **BF6y25pl3**

The downloaded filename will be **BFI-Level-1.zip**

Please note, the password will be changed at regular intervals so make sure you save a copy of the files once you have downloaded them.

We would advise you not to try to download the free digital files to a phone. Some of the files are large and some are also of a type not supported on phones.

If you experience any difficulties with downloading your files, please email info@brilliantpublications.co.uk and we will get back to you as soon as possible.

Depending on the speed of your internet and the size of the download, it may take some time for the download to complete. To avoid problems, please make sure that your computer does not go to sleep during the download.

Note: We test the software on PCs and Apple Macs, but there are too many different types of hardware in schools for us to be able to test it on every device owned by schools.

Photo-credits:
Images used under licence from **Fotolia.com** and **Shutterstock.com**. Other images used courtesy of **Absfreepic.com**, **Flickr.com**, **Pixabay.com** and **Tripadvisor.co.uk**

La France en couleurs:
Title page:	Traditional French colourful macarons; Pakhnyushchy; Shutterstock.com
Page 2:	Summer beach; Odpictures; Absfreepic.com
Page 3:	Aguille du Midi; Lucanne 78; Tripadvisor.com
Page 4:	Strawberries boxes baskets texture in outdoor market; Holbox; Shutterstock.com
Page 5:	Black Olives closeup. Selective Focus; Subbotina Anna; Shutterstock.com
Page 6, 9:	Grapes; Nightstar; Absfreepic.com
Page 7:	A field of sunflowers, in the south of France; Antonio Jorge Nunes; Shutterstock.com
Page 8:	Cityscape Paris; Marabu; Absfreepic.com
Page 9:	Normandie; CCraemer; Pixabay.com: Sunflower field; Jimmyfortune; Absfreepic.com

Un, deux, trois … soleil !
Title page:	Sandcastle, bucket and spade on beach; Rocklights; Fotolia.com
Page 2:	A girl taking picture in green bushes; Bander; Fotolia.com
Page 3:	Sandcastle, bucket and spade on beach; Rocklights; Fotolia.com
Page 4:	Two boys having fun in waterslide; V&P Photo Studio; Fotolia.com
Page 5:	Portrait of three little cyclists riding their bikes; Pressmaster, Shutterstock.com
Page 6:	Quatre basset; Sacha22; Fotolia.com
Page 7:	Entspannte Kanu-Tour; ARochau; Fotolia.com
Page 8:	Ice cream; Jeshoots; Pixabay.com
Page 9:	Two boys having fun in waterslide; V&P Photo Studio; Fotolia.com: Young girl eats ice cream; determined; Fotolia.com: Five kayaks; Isaacanchen; Pixabay.com: Huskies; Violetta; Pixabay.com

Des animaux importants:
Title page:	Elephant/Beaver; Marabu; Absfreepic.com Bear; Mary15; Absfreepic.com Bald eagle; Flyupmike; Absfreepic.com / Lion roaring; Rian; Absfreepic.com Cockerel; Odpictures; Absfreepic.com Turtle; Writer93; Absfreepic.com
Page 2, 9:	Rooster; Odpictures; ABSFreePic.com: Coq_France; Pict rider; Fotolia.com
Page 3:	Lion in Forest; Miyeon; Absfreepic.com: Drapeau des Flandres; Photonbleu; Fotolia.com
Page 4, 9:	Brown bear; Skeeze; Pixabay.com: Teddy bear; Rook76; Fotolia.com
Page 5:	Beaver; Sandrahauser2; Pixabay.com: Vector cartoon clip art illustration of a cute, happy cartoon beaver waving a Canadian flag and giving a thumbs up; Dolimac; Shutterstock.com
Page 6, 9:	Elephant; ajoheyho; Pixabay.com: Postage stamp Ivory Coast 1966 African Elephant, Animal; Laufer; Fotolia.com
Page 7:	Giant Tortoise; Redkite; Pixabay.com: Wall sculptures at Ngoc Son Temple; Chachanit; Fotolia.com
Page 8:	Bald eagle; Micakonrad; Pixabay.com: Majestic Bald eagle and USA flag; Ed Walls Photography; Shutterstock.com
Page 9:	Turtle; Writer93; Absfreepic.com: Lion King; Rebecca Wood; Flickr.com

Les jours de la semaine:
Title page:	Solar system; Matamu; Fotolia.com
Page 2:	Wolf howling in moonlight silhoutte; IFC; Fotolia.com
Page 3:	Mars; WikiImages; Pixabay.com: Antique gods Mars and Hermes in classical style; Eugenia Cherubini; Shutterstock.com
Page 4:	Mercury; WikiImages; Pixabay.com: Antique gods Mars and Hermes in classical style; Eugenia Cherubini; Shutterstock.com
Page 5:	Jupiter; WikiImages; Pixabay.com: Zeus, Jupiter or Jove from classical, Greek or Roman mythology wielding a lightning bolt / No meshes used; Christos Georghiou; Shutterstock.com
Page 6:	Red planet above the Earth's surface. Are there other planets like Earth? Combination of photo and 3D render; MarcelClemens; Shutterstock.com: Nascita di Venere. The birth of Venus (Botticelli); iralu; Shutterstock.com
Page 7:	Shabbat candles lighted; Lisa F. Young; Fotolia.com
Page 8:	Paris-Eglise:Vitrail; Atlantis; Fotolia.com
Page 9:	Wolf howling in moonlight silhoutte; IFC; Fotolia.com: Planet Mars with Rising Sun; Enrico G. Agostoni; Fotolia.com: Paris-Eglise:Vitrail; Atlantis; Fotolia.com

Bonjour, tout le monde !:
Title page:	Cute pupils smiling around a globe in classroom with teacher at the elementary school; Wavebreakmedia; Shutterstock.com
Page 2:	Large multi ethnic group of smiling young people saying hello; Markus Mainka; Fotolia.com
Page 3:	Handshake of two cheerful boys; SergiyN; Fotolia.com
Page 4:	和食食堂でアルバイトをする女性; Paylessimages: Fotolia.com
Page 5:	Greeting Indian woman; DragonImages; Fotolia.com
Page 6:	Love and togetherness; Lucky Dragon USA; Fotolia.com
Page 7:	Stick your tongue out in Tibet; Mchang. Mchang.net
Page 8:	High angle view of group of happy multiethnic people raising hands together; Bikeriderlondon; Shutterstock.com

C'est ça, Paris !:
Title page:	Eiffel Tower viewed from Paris Panoramic View; Moyen Brenn; Flickr.com
Page 2:	Eiffefl tower at Paris; Marabu; Absfreepic.com
Page 3:	Cityscape Paris; Marabu; Absfreepic.com
Page 4:	Montemartre; Ed Webster; Flickr.com
Page 5:	Musee Pompidou; bogitz; Pixabay.com
Page 6:	Chateau de Versailles, France; Philophoto; Fotolia.com
Page 7:	Notre Dame; Skeeze; Pixabay.com
Page 8:	Catacombes; Tdfugere; Pixabay.com
Page 9:	Catacombes; Skeeze; Pixabay.com: Sacre coeur at the summit of Montmartre, Paris; Pierre Leclerc; Shutterstock.com: Musee Pompidou; Alexandria; Pixabay.com: Eiffel Tower; Marbu; Absfreepic.com

Every effort has been made to trace copyright holders and to obtain their permission for the use of copyright material. The publisher apologizes for any errors or omissions in the above list and would be grateful for notification of any corrections that should be incorporated in future reprints or editions of this book.